P9-CIV-911

SCIENCE OF FUN STUFF

The Harlem Globetrotters Present the Points Behind Basketball

$$(a+b)^2 = a^2 + 2ab + b^2$$

$$S = a \times N$$

$$E = mc^2$$

Ready-to-Read

Simon Spotlight

New York London Toronto Sydney New Delhi

by Larry Dobrow

illustrations by Scott Burrough

SIMON SPOTLIGHT

An imprint of Simon & Schuster Children's Publishing Division

1230 Avenue of the Americas, New York, New York 10020

This Simon Spotlight edition August 2018

For information about special discounts for bulk purchases, please contact Simon & Schuster Special Sales at
1-866-506-1949 or business@simonandschuster.com.

Manufactured in the United States of America 0718 LAK

2 4 6 8 10 9 7 5 3 1

Library of Congress Cataloging-in-Publication Data

Names: Dobrow, Larry, author.

Title: The Harlem Globetrotters present the points behind basketball / by Larry Dobrow.

Description: Simon Spotlight edition. | New York : An imprint of Simon & Schuster Children's Publishing
Division, [2018] | Series: Science of fun stuff | Series: Ready-to-Read |
Includes a Science of Basketball Quiz. | Audience: Ages: 6-8.

Identifiers: LCCN 2017054063| ISBN 9781481487511 (paperback) | ISBN 9781481487528 (hardcover) |
ISBN 9781481487535 (eBook)

Subjects: LCSH: Basketball—Juvenile literature. | Harlem Globetrotters—Juvenile literature. |
Physics—Juvenile literature. | Newton, Isaac, 1642-1727—Juvenile literature.

Classification: LCC GV885.1 .D59 20108 | DDC 796.323—dc23 LC record available at
https://lccn.loc.gov/2017054063

CONTENTS

CHAPTER 1
Sir Isaac Newton, Basketball Sage

For almost one hundred years, the Harlem Globetrotters have been performing basketball plays and tricks that seem nearly impossible. They've played more than twenty-seven thousand games since being founded in the mid-1920s and have wowed fans in 123 countries and territories around the world. How do they make those four-point shots thirty feet away from the basket? How do they spin the basketball on just one finger for so long? How is it possible to jump high enough to dunk a basketball into a basket twelve feet above the floor?

One explanation for these amazing feats is science. Believe it or not, there's a whole lot of science going on behind the scenes of a basketball game. You have questions. Science has answers. So let's pull off the warm-ups and get out onto the court.

In order to explain the science of basketball, we have to go back in time to a person who lived two hundred years before basketball was even invented: Sir Isaac Newton. Newton was an English scientist who, in the year 1687, published the laws of motion. These laws inform just about everything regarding a basketball's path through the air and a player's movement on and around the court.

Newton's first law of motion states that, until a force acts on them, objects in motion will stay in motion. In other words, a moving object will continue moving until it is stopped by something.

But wait! When a player shoots a basketball, it doesn't stay in the air forever, even if it's the highest, most forceful shot possible. Something must bring the ball down, and that something is the force of gravity.

Gravity is the force that pulls objects toward each other. Gravity pulls on every object on Earth. The Earth is the largest object, so when a basketball is thrown into the air, gravity pulls it back to Earth.

$R_1 > 0$

R_2

But gravity isn't the only force helping to bring a basketball down. Something called "drag" is working to get the ball down too. The air around us might look empty, but there are actually tiny molecules that we can't see. They are moving in all different directions. Those molecules create drag by getting in the way of the ball and slowing it down.

Not all basketball shots are equal. Sometimes you only need to do a layup shot, and sometimes you have to make a four-point shot thirty feet from the basket. What determines how far a basketball will travel? That question leads us to Newton's second law of motion: The more force, or power, applied to an object, the more that object will speed up. So the longer the shot, the more force you will need to shoot.

Newton's third law of motion states that for every *action*, there is an equal and opposite *reaction*. This law is easy to understand using the example of a bouncing basketball. The *action* (the ball being dropped to the ground) prompts the *reaction* (the ball being pushed back up). The harder the force of the ball as it hits the ground, the higher it bounces back up.

CHAPTER 2
How to Make That Basket

There are many ways to make a shot in basketball. If you are shooting the ball into the air, as opposed to dunking (where the player brings the ball directly to the basket and pushes it in), one thing that is going to help you is getting backspin on the ball. This just means that the ball spins backward as it soars forward. Backspin helps the basketball slow down when it hits the rim or the backboard, and fall in the right direction. A slower ball is more likely to fall through the hoop than a faster ball, which will bounce farther away after it collides with the basket. The farther the rebound, the closer the ball will be to the other team's offensive side of the court, which is not what you want to have happen.

The force with which you need to throw a basketball into the air depends on the mass, or the weight, of the ball. The more mass an object has, the more force you need in order to throw it. Imagine you have two items to throw into a basket:

a basketball and a boulder. The boulder is heavier than the basketball, so you'll need to throw it harder to get it into the air. Thank goodness basketball isn't played with boulders!

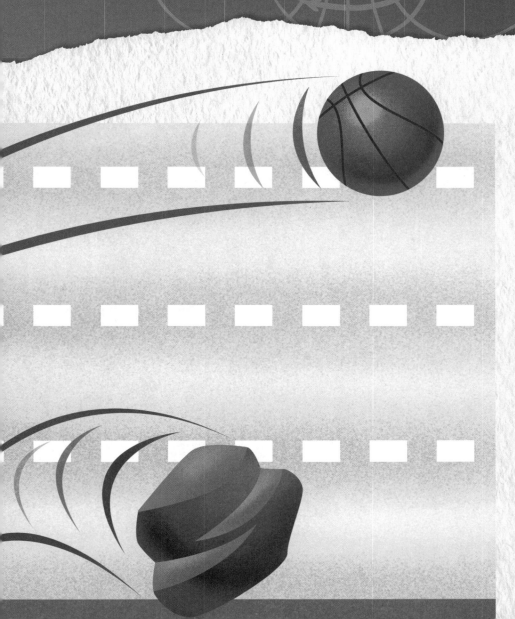

The speed of the basketball also depends on how hard it's thrown. Remember Newton's second law of motion: The more force applied to an object, the more that object will speed up? In other words, if you need to pass the ball to a teammate before the clock runs out, throw the ball with all the force you've got!

CHAPTER 3
The Physics Behind the Tricks

So now we know some of the basic
principles behind basketball shots.
But what about some of the Harlem
Globetrotters' most famous tricks? Maybe
science can help us answer the question
asked at every game: "How in the world
do they do that?"

One of the most famous tricks of the Harlem Globetrotters is spinning a basketball on one finger. Here's how it's done: First, you throw the ball into the air with some spin on it. Then you catch it on your index finger. As long as your index finger remains steady, the ball will keep spinning. This is due to another concept of physics called centripetal (sen-TRIP-i-tal) force, which is a force that pulls in toward the object's center. This keeps the ball upright and moving.

Another awe-inspiring part of a Harlem Globetrotters game is their incredible jumping skills. In 2000, Harlem Globetrotter Michael "Wild Thing" Wilson dunked a basketball in a net twelve feet up in the air. (The standard height of a basket is two feet lower—ten feet.) How does someone jump so high? Once again the answer can be found in physics. We'll start with Newton's third law. When a basketball player bends his or her knees and prepares to jump, his or her feet press down on the floor. This pressure is the action. An athlete can jump higher or lower depending on the speed at which he or she starts the jump. The reaction is that the floor responds by exerting an equal but opposite force.

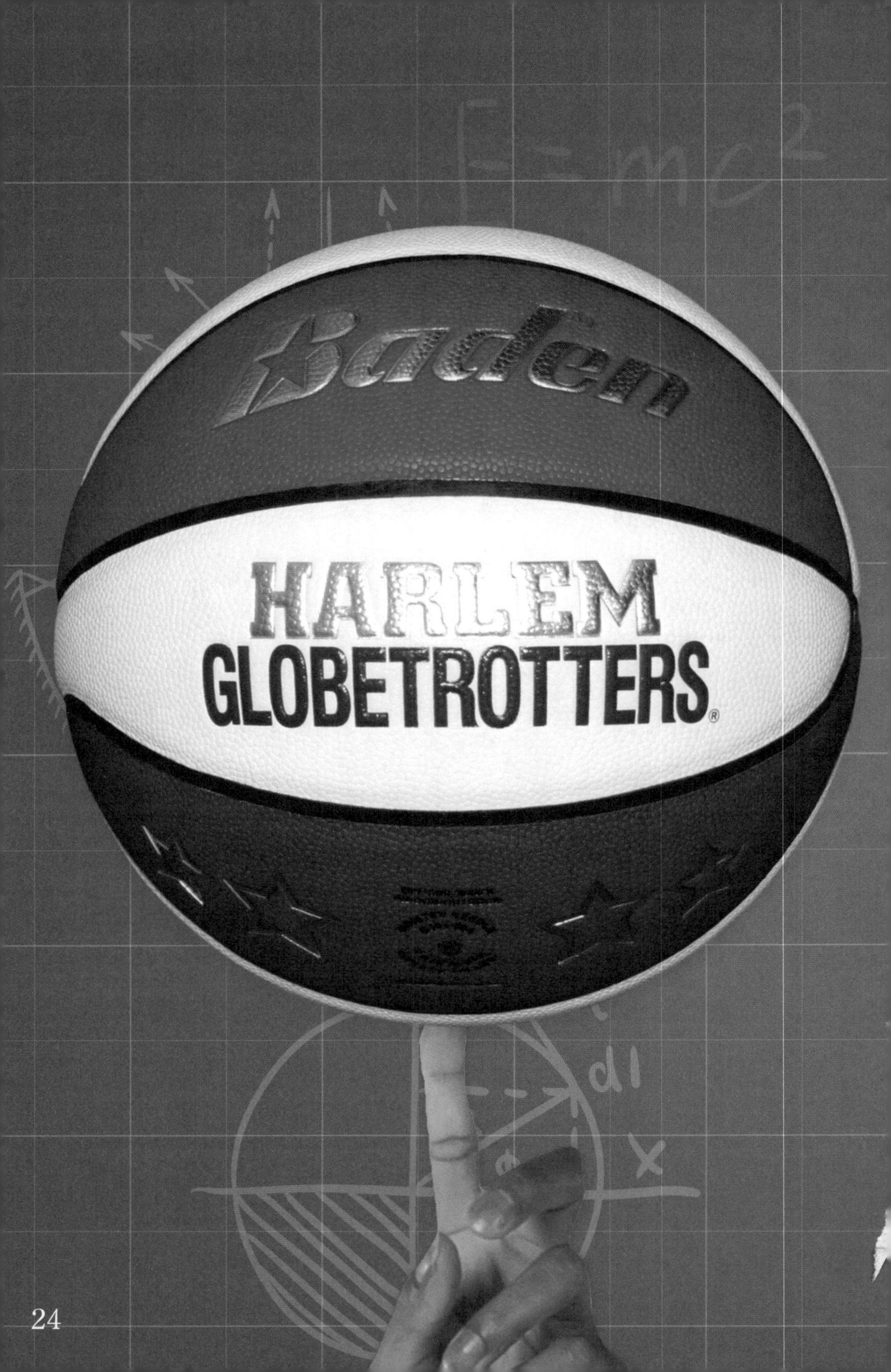
E=mc²
Baden
HARLEM
GLOBETROTTERS®
dl
x

CHAPTER 4
Inside the Basketball

So far, we've talked a lot about the physics of playing basketball, but what about the ball itself? What makes it suited to the game? To the untrained eye, there's nothing special about a basketball. It's round and it bounces, like any number of other sports balls. However, on closer inspection, basketballs are surprisingly complex.

The innermost layer of a basketball is called the inner bladder. This is a round ball made up of a really airtight material called butyl rubber. Butyl rubber is a

synthetic rubber made out of chemicals in a lab. This material is not only used in basketballs—it's also found in some car tires.

Once the rubber is shaped into the size of a basketball, a machine makes sure it stays that way by wrapping thread around

it. This thread is usually composed of
nylon or polyester, two synthetic materials.

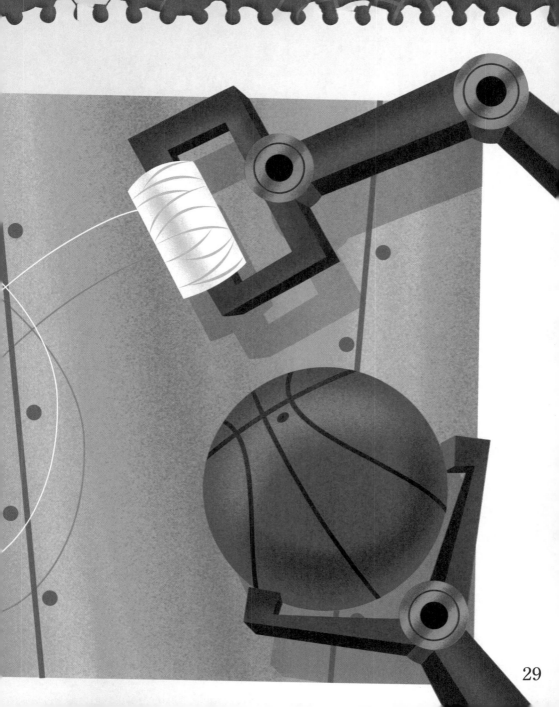

Finally, the best basketballs, such as the ones used by the Globetrotters, the National Basketball Association, the Women's National Basketball Association, and men's and women's college teams, have high-quality leather covers. Leather is easier to grip than other types of material. Playground basketballs tend to have either rubber or synthetic rubber covers. Some basketballs even have leather and rubber composite covers.

For leather-covered basketballs, the cover consists of panels stitched together with thread. For other kinds of basketballs, the panels are held in place with glue.

SCIENCE
OF FUN STUFF

EXPERT
ON
BASKETBALL

Congratulations! The buzzer has sounded, and you've come to the end of this book. You are now an official Science of Fun Stuff Expert on basketball. Impress your friends and family with all the cool things you know, and the next time you're at a game, remember all the science going on behind the scenes.

Hey, kids! Now that you're an expert on the science of basketball, turn the page to learn even more about natural rubber, Guinness World Records, and basketball careers!

Natural Rubber

Rubber is the tough but stretchy material that is used to make car tires, garden hoses, and rubber bands. Basketballs are made of synthetic rubber. Synthetic means that something is man-made and can't be found in nature.

Not all rubber is synthetic. Natural rubber is

found inside tropical trees in South America. We can collect it by tapping, or making small cuts into the bark of a rubber tree. A white liquid sap called latex drips out of the cut and into a bucket. After the sap is collected, it is coagulated (koh-AG-u-lay-ted), which is a fancy term for hardening a liquid into a solid. The natural rubber is then shipped to a factory and formed into its final shape.

World Records

The Harlem Globetrotters aren't just world-class basketball players—they are also world-class record holders! As of June 2018, the members of the Harlem Globetrotters hold sixteen Guinness World Records. (Guinness World Records keeps track of the most outstanding facts and figures in different categories. They update them every year to include new record breakers.) The list is sure to grow in the coming years!

1. **Highest Basketball Dunk:** 12 feet (record held by Michael "Wild Thing" Wilson)

2. **Most Basketball Three-Pointers in One Minute (Single Ball):** 10 shots each (Ant Atkinson and Cheese Chisholm)

Cheese Chisholm

3. **Longest Basketball Shot While Blindfolded:** 73 feet, 10 inches (Ant Atkinson)

4. **Most Underhanded Half-Court Shots in One Minute:** 6 shots (Buckets Blakes)

Bull Bullard

5. **Most Half-Court Shots Made in an Hour (Team):** 348 shots (Thunder Law, Hammer Harrison, Bull Bullard, Spider Sharpless, Buckets Blakes)

Ant Atkinson

6. **Most Bounced Basketball Three-Pointers in One Minute:** 5 shots (Zeus McClurkin)

7. **Most Slam Dunks in One Minute (Individual):** 16 dunks (Zeus McClurkin)

Zeus McClurkin

8. Longest Underhand Basketball Shot:
84 feet, 8.5 inches (Hammer Harrison)

Hammer Harrison

9. Longest Time Spinning a Basketball on the Nose:
7.7 seconds (Scooter Christensen)

10. Longest Basketball Hook Shot: 72 feet,
6.25 inches (Big Easy Lofton)

**11. Longest Blindfolded Basketball Hook
Shot:** 58 feet, 2.5 inches (Big Easy Lofton)

Big Easy Lofton

**12. Farthest Basketball Shot Made
Backward:** 82 feet, 2 inches (Thunder Law)

**13. Farthest Basketball Shot Under One
Leg:** 52 feet, 5.5 inches (Thunder Law)

**14. Farthest Basketball Shot Made While
Sitting on the Court:** 58 feet, 9.1 inches
(Thunder Law)

Thunder Law

15. Highest Upward Basketball Shot:
50 feet, 1 inch (Thunder Law)

**16. Most Countries Visited by a Basketball
Team:** 123 countries (Harlem Globetrotters)

Basketball Jobs

The Harlem Globetrotters team isn't just made up of professional athletes. They also have a large staff that works both on and off the basketball court. Which job would you like to try?

Referee

A referee makes sure that the athletes play fairly and follow the rules of the game.

Statistician

A basketball statistician works with data, like the number of free throws made in a game and turnovers per game. The information that a statistician calculates helps the team understand their strong and weak points. It also helps them decide which players to draft onto their team.

Athletic Trainer

Sometimes athletes get hurt when they play sports. An athletic trainer is a special medical professional who helps athletes recover from their injuries and get back on the court.

Photographer

A basketball photographer takes pictures that can be used in newspapers and on social media sites. Because of his or her job, a photographer gets the best views of the basketball game!

Being an expert on something means you can get an awesome score on a quiz on that subject! Take this

Science of Basketball Quiz

see how much you've learned.

1. Who was Sir Isaac Newton?

   a. the first Harlem Globetrotter

   b. the president of the NBA

   c. an English scientist

2. What causes a basketball to fall to the ground when it's in the air?

   a. gravity and drag   b. hang time   c. action and reaction

3. Which law of motion explains how a basketball bounces?

   a. Newton's first law   b. Newton's second law   c. Newton's third law

4. Which force helps keep a basketball upright when it's spinning on one finger?

   a. gravity   b. mass   c. centripetal force

5. What will help you make a long four-point shot?

   a. a faster ball   b. a heavier ball   c. an oval-shaped ball

6. Why is backspin important?

   a. It hurts less if the ball hits an athlete.

   b. It slows the ball down.

   c. It makes the ball bounce higher.

7. Where is synthetic rubber made?

   a. in forests   b. in labs   c. in caves

8. What material do the Harlem Globetrotters use for their basketball covers?

   a. leather   b. rubber   c. plastic

Answers: 1.c 2.a 3.c 4.c 5.a 6.b 7.b 8.a